CHEERS MATE
I'll give it a GO!

Jottin's of a Jovial Jotter

Written and Illustrated
by
Ray Chapman

Published by:
ARTHUR H. STOCKWELL LTD
Torrs Park   Ilfracombe   Devon
Established 1898
www.ahstockwell.co.uk

LD 3982151X

The reader of this poem will need a normal 'English' voice; Gwendoline has a 'well-brung-up' gentry voice; and the farmhand has a Devonshire accent.

Enough Said

Ms Gwendoline Amphlett Bristow-Browne
Lay in a ditch, all upside down.
Was not until farmhand Oswald Gerrard Isaiah Kite
Came riding by and saw her bike,
Stopping then for close inspection,
Observed two legs with waving action.

" It be a damn good thing the fabric's tough.
Be it man-made or that drat silken stuff ?"
She said, " Really ! . . . You lecherous bore,
Go ! Phone Mummy from the store."
Stepping off, turned his bike around,
She screamed, " First help me out, you grinning hound !"

He said, " What ? " . . . She said, " You !"
He said, " Not like that with all that goo.
In this heat, 'n' flies a-buzzin'
You look like spotted dick wrapped up in muslin.
I'll come back with this mate of mine –
We'll be finished muck-spreadin' . . . 'bout 'alf past nine.

He has a lorry, and a tank for water;
Time we're done, Mum won't know her daughter.
You lay there, you'll soon smell of pine."
She said, " Naff off ! " . . . He said, " Fine ! "

This poem is better read to the music from the English film
Restoration (Track 17: 'Katherine Sleeps').

A Welcome Is from Our Household Gone

Upon reflection,
Two months back
Bonnie became distressed.
Two months ago,
Two months ago,
Back . . . along . . . life's track.

Walks became much shorter –
Bonnie, always keen to go.
After half . . . then down to minutes,
She didn't want to know.

For our loyal, loving . . . West Highland white
Breathing became a chore –
Naturally, sent us scurrying
To the veterinary's door.

Her sides would pump –
Her heart still strong, . . . even to the last.
Sitting, looking at her vet,
His judgement had been passed.

After loves 'n' whispers, " Thank you . . . Sorry, Bon,"
Decision left to us.
" You could bring her back tomorrow, but the cancer
Plus the fluid" . . . . . . words we had to trust.

Bonnie's fifteen and a half years' faith in humans
Proven many times, . . . by trust.
She looked . . . she sank . . . into supportive arms,
She sleeps, . . . having still the faith in us.

Dropping the H's is definitely intentional.

'acked out for Ever
or
It's 'er – what's 'er name ? . . .

Started in a sculptor's studio
With 'er up there on the stand ;
She was looking rather wobbly –
I offered her my hand.
She said, " This honour, it appeals to me –
I'll be all right in a mo'.
It means I'll never put on weight –
Being sculpted, put on show."

So, hop up on this pedestal
Only for a minute
While they 'ump the granite in,
To see if he can fit you in it.
YES ! . . . It's about to happen –
From granite you'll be 'acked,
Perched upon a pedestal –
What'cher think of that ?

I bet you're so excited
To be set up on display,
To stand 'acked out for ever
In a meadow out the way.
Not too far ! – you will be seen
From the flyover, and in between,
Far enough to avoid the fumes,
Near the junction, where the Visitors, Centre, looms.

You know best, the summer dress
To grab for sex appeal;
You know best, the winceyette vest
For wearing in a field.
For on the ridge, on winter nights,
There lurks Everard Pete.
Did you know 'e has a fetish
For sucking frozen feet ?

The actual sculpture will not take long –
He's a clever sculpting fella.
He's thrown out his mallet
And bought a power hammer.
He got fed up with tap 'n' chip,
Cash flow dropped to nil;
Thought he'd better speed it up,
Now he can't stay still !

Every year the fan club
(If we can get them out the pub)
Will 'ike, with banners waving
To give this bird a scrub.
Buckets, mops, steps 'n' sprays –
They may look a motley lot –
Then the veteran shouted:
" Who chose this blasted spot ?"

From the side, someone said with pride,
" She be really quite a gal,
Cos then when I knew 'er
She always scrubbed up well."
You'll be granted freedom of the parish –
Guess you know your way around.
This could pose a problem
With the housewives of the town.

They may not always be alert
As you wander freely down each track.
You may by chance glimpse a housewife
As she scrubs 'er 'usband's back.
Not that he'd be worried
If he's sitting in the tub;
But if his wife's distracted,
They would hear him at the club.

In years to come a council gang,
As the cracks appear,
They won't be using ointment,
It'll be sealant ! – did you hear ?
You will be amongst the famous –
Nelson had a dose,
Standing with all those birds around,
Cracked earlier than most.

After the unveiling
And supper at the hall
There will be one function pending –
The Lord Mayor's Multicultural Ball.
His Worship is bewildered,
Council sat all night –
They have one remaining problem:
The townsfolk now want 'er within their sight.

Most it seems don't want 'er stood
'acked out on the moor,
They want 'er in the city square,
To ogle and adore –
A place to sit with sandwiches,
Names engraved upon each seat,
Chuck chunks 'n' bits of their lunch
In front of people's feet.

Problem being – to quote
A St Aldgates counter clerk
" It's 'iggins, the town crier,
'e's such a blinkin' twerp
Now it's known why he proposed the spot.
Security ! – it's near my 'ouse," he said.
The only clue his wife gave –
He could see her from his bed !

This of course was resolved –
Boys will have their day.
There was one small distraction –
Had to drag 'iggins away.
" You won't get it ! You won't find it !"
Unbeknown to 'im, they 'ad
Found the ceremonial tarpaulin
In a shed owned by his dad.

Results are in from our opinion poll.
" It looks a lot like 'er, even to the smile.
I recognised the stance as 'ers,
Back there, 'bout a mile."
Strange why she was never named –
'is 'ammer must have slipped.
Maybe was the money
And couldn't afford that bit.

It's gaining in popularity,
They want one in 'ackney Wick.
The Dean of 'arrow, 'e's been on –
How can we cope with it ?
'ang about, fax is churning out . . .
'arlow, 'arbledown, 'arescombe,
'ampstead, 'eyshott, 'orning –
Even 'ard Knott Pass.

They won't be getting granite –
They'll get the rest in fibreglass !

All the Way from Aussie

My search for Pam the Writer
Began at the village pub,
In 'at with corks, moleskin shorts,
Complete with Diners Club.

Leaning on the counter,
As patrons' eyes narrowed to a squint
I bail up the publican, ask,
" Do you know this writer you have up here in print ?"

Landlord shouts, " GET OUT !
I know your type – I'll not put her in.
You blasted paparazzi lot
Need some discipline.

" Take your camera – disappear !
Before I thump you hard !
You'll get no shots of her, mate,
'cos she never goes that far."

" I'm no Continental
With a whopping lens ;
I'm from here, come back home
And, hopefully, make friends.

" I've flown all the way from Aussie –
Please give me a clue."
" Have ya now ? Good to hear –
It's the Duck Pond, blue, for you !"

Grabbed from every angle,
Some – not all – discreet,
Soon found myself floundering
In the 'muck pond' 'cross the street.

Happened all so quickly –
I struggle from the pond,
Bump ! into a yokel, wrapped around
A short 'n' rotund blonde ! . . .

He said, " You seem bewattled, zur.
Puff on this, you'll see;
Then we kud go together
'n' see if she see me."

Faced with a translation problem
Vibrating in my ears,
Said, " I need a good scrub-up
In case sweet Pam appears."

Glancing up across the road,
I see the vicar waving.
He must have heard my plea
As I stand dripping on the paving.

" Here, take these clothes, have a shower,
Change into them, my son,"
Said the vicar, scooting off –
He was off to see his mum.

How do I reach this lady ?
The postie, 'e would know
This famous local writer,
With all his to 'n' fro.

I'll pop into the post office,
Write a little note,
Tuck Pam's in, then
One for 'im on the envelope.

" Dear Mr Postman, you have style, charm,
An obliging friendly face –
Would you find Pam the Writer ?
You would know her place.

" I've come all the way from Aussie
To contact Pam the Poet.
Whistle a song, you'll whiz along,
So, on yer bike, 'n' toe it !"

Big-End Muddle with Greasy Jen's Double

Have you ever waved to someone – by mistake?
Pull your arm down fast, maybe, fake an ache!
See, I thought this girl was Jen,
Who screamed, " Was you waving at me then?"
Said, " I'm sorry – human error – wrong big end."

I was certain she was Jen, who works the pump.
No wonder, as I waved, she got the 'ump.
Could have sworn it was Jen's posterior –
Knickers, never clearer,
Through the trousers that she wears,
Although she's plump!

Jen's a happy, easy-going type of girl,
Seen her husband? Cripes! – he's big – his name is Earl.
Although most teeth are missing,
It's been said he's good at kissing,
The only anchor being one tooth of pearl!

Seriously, I was sure she was Jen, who pumps the juice.
Some give her fat a pinch, if it is loose!
Jen has a red Barina, rosy cheeks –
You must have seen her.
Do you stop by often at this dump?

Jen's a character – always wants to please;
Holds the caps from various cars between her knees.
It's a system that she has – be it petrol, oil, gas,
Leaves me spellbound how she finds them with such ease.

Usually, Jen has a lot to say.
If one is quick, the air hose is fair play –
Poke it down her trousers –
Stops her gassing there for hours.
To pull it out may take another day!

The difference being . . . .

Between that bird 'n' Jen,
Jen wears runners, she wore Ugg boots – comprehend ?
Although they both wear trousers,
Jen's have grease on, hers have flowers,
Tho' their crimplene pants would certainly fit Big Ben !

I will stop – I can see you are bemused.
How could I mistake someone such as you ?
Crikey ! you resemble Jen.
You've not popped back again.
Different clobber, I'm in bother – same big end !

The usher in this poem has a West Country accent.

Biscuits, Tea . . . and Sir John B.

Outside Sir John Betjeman's Memorabilia Room
There are depressing blocks of grey,
Depressing blocks of people,
All depressed in their own way.

Inside, proud and cosy,
Tea room down the hall.
Absorbing first the foyer,
" Need help, sir ? " came the usher's call.

" A busier spot in J.B.'s time, sir !
Sounds of 'Case, sir ?' steam, then whistle,
Bustle, bags 'n' trolleys
Where porters once did bristle.

" In this restored ex-railway station, sir,
Listen: " Wadebridge ! Wadebridge ! " echoes off the walls.
" Please mind the doors. This way, sir,"
Usher softly calls.

" I met Sir John, I shook his hand."
" Really ? Which hand did you use ? "
" My right one, sir ! "
" Well, put it here – that's the one I'll choose."

" This, sir, is Sir John's room.
Most treasured things are here: his desk, his chair,
His cap, his gown. Sadly, Archibald left with John,
Both beyond repair."

" We have a Teddy Sit-In, always 'whispered' in this room.
If you care to reminisce, tea and biscuits will be along."
A chair is placed, a table flipped . . . [*pause*].
" Oh ! the video, sir, is only twenty minutes long."

ARCHIBALD, J.B.'s toy bear since childhood is buried with him at St Enodoc Church, Cornwall. The resident bear (in a glass case) is a sit-in of the same type as the original.
I visited there on Tuesday 6th March 2001.

Blow a Kiss to England
(For a Friend Living in Guernsey)

A favour, plea, no great expense,
More a thought, plus deed,
Simple, easy, graphic –
This we both agreed.
PLEASE,
Blow a kiss to England
from
Your Guernsey home.
Take time, with love
Lest we forget
Her torment as we roam.
I'm thinking now of her earth,
Tortured
Land and Fen.
Stop, consider, blow a kiss,
PLEASE,
Once more, again.
Flint stone walls,
Secure, deep,
Hold red boxes
Firm to keep.
Badgers' sett, burrowing mole,
Darling, sweet George,
Up a pole –
Images your island
Is familiar with.
Touch a thorn bush,
Disturb a wren.

EMOTIONAL,
I'll start again:
PLEASE,
Blow a kiss to England,
This I do implore.
I dread to think what can erupt,
Disturb
Her gentle core.
PLEASE,
Blow a kiss to England
Whilst you're near her shore.
Direct a tear,
with intent,
As many have before.

Car Boot Sales and Cowpats

Car boot sales and cowpats,
Normally acres apart,
Over in Devon, England –
These are movements close to thine 'eart !

Field it is host
To a collective of pats,
Some protected by stalls,
Others covered with mats.

Those in the open,
Between buyers and stalls,
May have bunting around
To deter any sprawls.

Folk sidestep 'n' cross
At this grand cowpat dance –
Sort of hopscotch gone rural,
A mere 'Dance of Chance'.

Pause for a moment
At the Bric-a-Brac stall.
You may feel you're shorter
Where once you were tall.

A few folk head for
'Ye Olde Hot Dog Stand' –
Have their senses gone troppo
To blend with the 'Smell of the Land' ?

It's so hard to tell.
Many a farm person here –
Have they all been muck-spreadin',
Or is a trailer too near ?

Stop at the cheese stall –
A ' Whiff ' quickly . . . arose ! –
A Rose slightly different –
A . . . Gorgonzola, . . . suppose ?

I came here to rummage,
I now need a trough.
I've collected more than my share –
I must wash it off !

[*Fade*] . . . I say, can I borrow your bucket ?
Where's the nearest tap, please ?
Right over where ?
Gawd ! . . . OK . . . ta !

Chickens That Lay Jumbos

Jumbo eggs ! – you've heard of them –
Not ELEPHANT, OSTRICH or GOOSE.
It's CHICKENS ! . . . WOT LAYS 'EM –
They're either caged-in or run-loose.

The real clue to look for
When buying these 'ens
Is a very small 'ead
With very . . . 'BIG ENDS !'

The breed you would know them
Their eyes start to squint,
They pretend to squat down,
They then . . . stand up and SPRINT !

They parade for a while . . .
When they're ready to lay,
Then walk round in a circle,
. . . Then all walk away !

You'll hear a little short 'SQUARK',
They will WINCE . . . CLUCK . . . 'n' STOP.
Their 'ead sort of TWITCHES
And the EGGS, they just . . . DROP.

The birds look bewildered
Then 'PROP' on their beaks –
It's the best bit of timing,
Took only . . . . . . THREE TWEAKS !

Birds happy, contented,
Chirp a few bars.
After landing a JUMBO
They then see the stars.

The 'ens may then 'lay back',
Legs kicking cool air,
Head bends between them –
See if it's one or a pair.

They may not have feeling,
Tend, to lay on one side,
Leaving, their, . . . Big Ends
Glowing . . . with pride !

Flashback to the Outback
OR
What an Answering Service Can Do for You

G'd 'ay ! . . . I'm phoning yoos from Aussie.
             I'm in 'me' thongs 'n' vest.
             I'm holdin' up me stubby –
Cheers ! . . . thought you'd be impressed.

             I have this little message
             For your presenter now on Two,
             I tell yers I was 'Bushwhacked'
             To hear . . . " Keep it short " 'n' " That'll do."

Now . . . . . . it's been a real long time, BLUE,
             Since a Sheila said that to me.
             The last time I remember was
             As I dropped 'me' bike in '93.

             She was working in a paddock
             On the other side of scrub;
             She didn't speak great English
             But, I tell yers, flies flew off me hub.

             I hadn't even noticed her
             Working quietly, plump and short.
             I stood there . . . Counting Berries !
             Not thinking, I'd be caught .

             A 'similarly', you Poms would call it,
             As in London sends excitement through yer spine.
             I stopped what I was doing –
             . . . Her gloves were full of lime !

Flight of Fancy

I watched her walk in as we boarded the plane.
Her legs, her thighs, her manner
As I stowed my bag, in the locker above
Convinced . . . she was there to enamour.

She turned to sit down, making no sound.
She was here, sitting, healthy and able.
I chance a glance – her alluring smile ! –
My laptop became then . . . unstable.

Her perfume, her hair, her jewellery, . . . her knees –
She has 'The Presence' that leads man to trouble.
It wasn't until . . . Twelve Hours had passed
There was more than a hint of . . . fresh stubble !

How could I be sure, it's so rude to stare !
Decorum – she's nobody's fool.
Then as she rose . . . 'To Powder' . . . who knows ? –
She had to be two metres tall !

At twenty minutes past two came a hullabaloo
Down the aisle, outside the loo.
Was then 'HE' appeared, Lipstick . . . up round his ear.
Sighed, " I smacked them ! I can do it for you !

" Well, my smooth Porcelain Head, my name is Ted.
It's been a thrill observing your glances."
He blew kisses all round. Three stewards were found,
Inspired . . . by his graphic advances.

I have this to add: when confined in a plane
'PERVIN'S' . . . the wrong thing to do
Because . . . because . . . Cor, well, blinkin' 'ell,
A 'BEAUTY' may sit next to YOU !

Has Anyone Seen 'er Magnum Opus ?

Dear Lady,
With total honesty I do write.
I've looked 'n' poked to seek,
Been in malls,
Looked on stalls –
Even up our street.

I bet you're wondering
'What's all this ?
WOTS 'e looking for ?
Not another whinging Pom !
Met blokes
Like 'im before.

Where is it, madam?
Who's got it tucked
Hidden, out of sight?
Where is your 'magnum opus'?
I missed out on
'PLAYHOUSE Night'?

I had hope of buying one.
The foyer –
Took a while to complete
From my seat in the stalls
. . . LEVEL . . .
With your feet!

As time progressed
I reach the door.
Attendant appeared polite
Until he said,
" YOU'LL BE CHUFFED AT THE BACK
WE'VE SOLD THE LOT TONIGHT! "

Yes, I have enquired –
It's taken five months, at least,
. . . or Three!
I would so much like to read it.
Would you bring one here to Aussie?
. . . I'LL PROVIDE THE TEA!

If You Should Choose to Visit 'azel When Convalescing Here at 'ome
or
"ELLO!"

The Hoover is in the laundry,
An upright yellow beast;
Tea and coffee in the kitchen
Next to the tin marked 'yeast'.

Sheets, Undies, Towels 'n' stuff
Are in the washing machine;
Follow the instructions,
Hang out when they're clean.

The snipper and the mower
Are bordering on antique;
Give both a kick, then a shake –
They'll be at their peak.

Thursday being 'Bin Collection',
Should you call this day,
It's two bins out every other week;
The rest can . . . blow away.

Containers stacked up in the fridge
Appear to have gathered fur;
If I move 'em round, or stack 'em up,
They shoot back . . . all a blur.

Hazel is advised not to lift –
No more than a cup –
Reason being 'A Ladies Thing'
Although she's on the up.

So basically I've given in.
With Nutella, Chips 'n' Cheese,
Plus eating chocolate raisins
Has brought me to 'me' knees.

I've an 'eadache now, and 'Done 'me' back',
Feeling rather weak . . .
Should you need me at all
I'll be . . . painting by the creek !

Lust for Life in the Morgue

Gloria was cleaning the slab,
Realised her job is so drab.
She soon sprang to life
When a chap with a knife
Gave a quick wink, made a grab.
He asked her to tap dance, it seems –
A pathologist, well stacked, forty-three;
Table polished and gleaming,
Stainless steel – what a feeling ! –
Gloria pulled herself up with all speed.

Her uniform press studs, they popped.
He simply stood static, lip dropped,
His mouth was agape.
She shouted: " DO YOU HAVE A TAPE ! ?
Or will you whistle a tune from the top ?"
Within seconds, he let out a sigh –
For him on the floor time was nigh.
Unbeknown to her,
The reflection transferred
Up as far as a sweet butterfly.

He said, " Is the tattoo a clue to the tune ?"
She jumped down, grabbed a mop very soon,
Hit him under the chin.
He was small, very thin.
Was then he ran out of the room !
Gloria, observed, looking down,
Was perplexed. Said to herself with a frown,
" How could I possibly, TAP !
Up there for the chap ?
WHITE WELLIES don't make the right sound !"

Pamela Potters in Her Garden

Pamela Potters in her garden –
Not the Potter you may know,
This Pamela lives near Axminster
Coining in the dough.

Pam had a Richmond rooftop garden
Not far from Heathrow.
Found shadows of low-hovering jets
'er vegies wouldn't grow !

Pamela now potters here, potters there,
Watching acres of 'em grow,
Dividing clumps of pretty plants
With her WHOPPIN' . . . NEW . . . BACKHOE.

Well, you know how some folks garden –
Sensitive sort of souls –
Pamela keeps the wildlife occupied,
Wedging rocks into their 'oles !

Bugs 'n' frogs 'n' delightful birds
Sit gasping on the lawn,
Longing for a fish pond
'cos, the bird bath's long since gawn !

Mr Shale arrives every day –
Lives off the beaten track !
He'll flip the mighty compost heap
Then start on his way back.

Midst the bushes and wildlife
Pam prefers to potter,
Up 'er jumper always keeps
A pen and spiral jotter.

Pam she is a writer –
She needs this quiet relief,
Never forgets her husband,
Always takes him in a leaf.

'cos if the telly's boring,
He rehearses for his part
As Adam, in the Job Centre's, production,
" *We're in the Apple Cart.*"

Last weekend,
Pamela, thinking it worthwhile,
Gave Mr Shale a 'Business Break'
To 'make another pile' !

With fruits and vegies in the van
Off to the local market
Mr Shale drove back again –
There was nowhere he could park it !

" Oh ! Mr Shale ! you've returned !"
Cried Pamela, running down the path.
" Now calm down, Pam. What 'ave you found ?"
He said, trying not to laugh.

" Well, I was looking at me cucumbers . . ."
Mr Shale, he tried to calm her.
Pam, in shock, blurted out,
" He was there – some half-dressed, demented farmer !"

Mr Shale repaired the gap
The nasty man came through.
As one can well imagine,
There was quite a 'BIG t' DO'.

Peace restored, Pam still explores
Dark corners her garden has to offer.
Secretly she hopes to find
A bloke that doesn't cost 'er !

Passion Perks

Years of pollution Budge sucked in.
Make-up, powder, fumes from gin.
Feathers lay in the dust
As Molly wrestled with her bust.

A variety girl, . . . one may say,
Friend to all . . . to this day –
Molly seldom considers Budge
Except to give his cage a nudge.

Never noticed yellow, curling beak
When she prompted him to speak.
Budge's cage gave a lurch,
Tiny feet gripped the perch.

Moll, attempting to pull on her tights,
Had given Budge another fright.
All in all, too much to *bare* –
Moll sat down in her underwear.

Picking up her filter tips,
Rammed one in between her lips.
Her swinging earrings, twice Budge's size,
Had Budge swaying, mesmerized.

This, of course, was now to end
As Moll picked up another friend –
A big fat cat, a Persian cross,
Given name: Passion Boss.

Passion Boss gave Budge a wink;
Budge tottered over for a drink.
Budge had faith in Boss's plan
As Boss sat with Moll on her divan.

Passion Boss, when a younger cat,
Played a part in Molly's act;
Sometimes performed upon a stage,
Though private room was all the rage.

Moll's innocent victims of passive smoking
Thought, 'It's ol' Moll we should be choking –
Smoking forty cigs a day
For many favours, plus her pay.'

Smoke from cigs swirled round Budge's cage,
Turned easy-going Budge into a rage.
He rang his bell, shook his door –
Finally Budge could take no more.

Although exhausted, saw no escape,
Budge feebly shouted, " Rape ! Rape ! Rape !'
Molly taken by surprise,
As nylon lace pinched her thighs.

Molly now at sixty-one
Displayed a rump that weighed a ton.
In Slippers, Bra, Wig askew,
Boss thought this to be his cue.

Leaping up onto Moll's butt,
Claws gripped elastic round her gut.
Releasing this with a thwack !
Jumped from there into a hat.

This routine, once Moll bent over,
Boss learnt from a Turk . . . Moll met in Dover.
Passion Boss, now up and running
To a spot that let no sun in.

Tail erect whilst en route
Molly now let out a hoot
Running swift between Moll's legs,
Skidded . . . on her 'TOOTHY PEGS' !

Waking Budge from his slumber –
Budge thought this a different number.
Knowing not, which may be worse,
Budge swung into . . . original verse.

" WINDOW, WOMAN ! Need some air ! or divided we will fall. . . ."
Budge was interrupted as a slipper hit the wall.
Moll sat weeping, lit a Cig,
Remembering . . . 'BIG SAM'S' . . . one-legged jig.

'twas from Big Sam, Budge learnt this line
Only Big Sam made Moll's eyes shine
'cos every week, stepping from his Rolls-Royce MOTA,
Sam fulfilled . . . Moll's every quota.

Moll had sensed Sam's passion failing.
As for her pets, they weren't complaining.
Things have changed; over this past week
Moll's associate has reached his peak.

In Big Bold type, in Tabloid press:
" TOBACCO CHIEF DUMPS HIS MADAM FOR BARONESS ".
Molly, calm, began to grin
Said, " KEEP YOUR CIGS . . . I've a friend in GIN ! "

Poor Al Kida

Poor Al, he's a timid bloke,
Wouldn't harm a Blow-ee
Lived all his life in Ripple Creek
Just the other side of MOE   [Mo-ee].
September 9th 2001: Exploding planes and buildings,
Al's photo flashed near and far
As Federal Police surrounded him
Spraying foam all round his Jaguar.

Blaring out through car loudspeakers:
" Freeze ! Al Kida, freeze !"
Al could not understand: as the day was hot,
Who would choose to freeze ?
He Al Kida – (K-I-D-A), was he the one to blame ?
Al could only remember, when in bed with his current Sheila
The only thing exploding then was the lust he felt
And the goings-on between her.

Al, a terrorist ? Certainly not !
Was far too hard and risky.
Al preferred to live his life on lamb kebabs,
Seducing girls he'd ply with whisky !
Al, a citizenship-wielding Aussie lad –
Bleached hair in mullet style,
A proud survivor of unpaid traffic fines
Helps make his life worthwhile.

Al, being a country lad,
Never wished this much attention
When ordered to appear in court,
Pending investigation
As to why his shed half full of fireworks,
Plus three wives he forgot to mention.
Al broke down and blabbed this out,
Adding, " Two more are in detention."

Poor Al – poor, poor, poor Al
He was sure they'd never find 'er,
His last true love, wife number six,
Aasiya Soona Kida.

Tarquin's Trip of Trips to the Hotel Windsor

Tarquin, Tarquin's mummy, cousin, and Auntie Prue
Thought, 'Tea at the Windsor ? Yes ! that'll do.
Yes, that'll be right, I'm sure. That'll do.
It's somewhere today where we won't have to queue.'

" Tarquin, come here. Hold Mummy's hand.
No, no more paper pellets for your 'lastic band.
You stand here while I help Auntie Prue
Carry the stroller and bags, into this . . . 'owd yer do."

" I'm the concierge, madam." " Well, your not *ERGE*-in' me !"
As Tarquin ran by, with a small pot of tea,
Bumping Aunt Prue, on whose chest baby was wetting,
Tarquin then tripped – destroyed a whole table setting.

OH ! LOOK AT THIS STAIN ! LOOK at the mess !
Waitress is watching – put her off, I guess.
Tarquin's now running round with his trousers undone !
What's he got ? A large current bun !
That's Tarquin, Tarky, *my* son !   [*proudly*]

" Madam ! Madam ! Please step over here.
Strollers and nappy bags spoil the ambience, the décor, I fear."
" Spoils the what ? How about Prue ?
She'll need to breastfeed Sebastian in a minute or two !

" Tarquin ! Sebastian can't eat your delicious cream scone.
Tarquin ! Take it away !
Mummy's sorry to shout, but he's starting to foam !
Tarquin ! Tarquin ! Gawd ! where's he gone ?"
" Madam, please hurry, he's approaching the gong.

" Madam, he's seen you – pulled over a plant.
Madam, control him – I'm not arrogant.
He's running towards us with a full plate of jam
Topped with Ricketts ice cream and a few scraps of ham.

" Madam, Auntie, having never been here before,
Traditional tea, this time of day, is in dollars up near the door."
" Dollars ? Door ? How much could it be ?"
" Under normal conditions, you, thirty-five;
Kid under twelve, . . . a mere twenty-three.

" Madam, dear madam, tho' hard to conceive,
He's tipping tea dregs over a valued guest's sleeve.
Madam, each of his fingers supports one chocolate eclair,
And has sat a banana peel on Lady Smythe's hair.

" Madam, he's livid, having been caught.
He'd pulled out, Sebastian's nappy and is pouring on salt !"
" Tarky, you're *naughty* ! No, Mummy didn't mean that.
You're only eleven, still Mummy's angel, still Mummy's pet *brat* !"

" Madam, your bill's in the vicinity of four hundred and three.
You haven't sat down or had any tea.
I strongly suggest that when next you arrive,
You leave Tarky, in a *secured* play area, till around 5.45."

Op Shop 'opefuls

I found a little Op shop
With menfolk queuing up.
It had a 'Red-Light' special on
Plus 'ot soup in a cup.

A few suspicious likely lads
Started to push in,
Thinking that 'The Christian Front'
Was trading now in sin.

Sin itself was not inside,
Neither was the Vicar.
He'd surreptitiously slipped out the back,
Clutching half a knicker.

Whilst inside this op shop,
Curtain rail running hot –
This we know is necessary
To stop folk seeing what you've got.

Through the front the vicar came –
He knew trade was patchy.
He hadn't wasted any time;
He'd been out for a 'Scratchie'.

He'd scooped a win,
Claiming God gave him the nod.
All the customers in the shop thought hard:
'Who is this bloke named God ?'

Chocolate biscuits, Irish cream –
Ol' Vic knew how to lay it on.
These hapless souls with stomachs full
Were being . . . 'Primed' . . . for evensong.

Salcombe to Frog Stone

Starting through woodland,
Sea seen sparkling through,
Sweet smells in shadow –
A wood with a view.

Rocky flint path
Leads down through a copse;
Out from the hawthorn
A young rabbit hops.

Pass through a gateway,
Dog at one's heel;
Life is so precious
As one nears the hill.

Leaf beetle crossing,
Missed by a toe;
It frantically scrambles,
Not sure – friend or foe ?

Stop ! view is stunning,
Framed, down between trees,
Sheep gently bleating,
No bigger than fleas.

We thought this breathtaking,
Yet in the next field
Young lambs were feeding,
Ewes proud of their yield.

Beach, fifteen inches,
Way down below;
Some folk have made it –
How ? I don't know.

Clouds gently rolling –
A view to behold –
This spells ENGLAND
For those of the mould.

Walkers appear:
Silence then gone.
Two seconds later,
Blackbird in song.

Thatched cottage; a farm
Set back in the combe;
Clouds gently rolling
Reveal nature's room.

Reader needs to develop a Cockney old boy 'spittle' voice.

Stumpy Saunders

I'm a straightener-up of 'ouses that are tilting.
Wiv jacks 'n' blocks 'n' 'ammer I'll explore.
When I'm tucked up under, I'll knock out a little number
'cos, I've got rhythm when I 'ammers on the floor.

The folk above like to know I'm working –
Makes 'em feel safer to know a 'stumper' such as me is 'darn' below.
Wiv 'me' trusty mallet, 'me' spade, I'll soon be at it,
Then I'll be up there with me hand out for the dough.

I'm the Senior Stump Setter-upper in the area.
Measures them from a scar up near 'me' thigh.
For other prime dimensions I use me 'ead 'n' arm in sections;
Then I lay back and measures 'em wiv 'me' eye.

It's been 'me' life – re-stumping what's gone rotten.
I'm nudging forty-two, I'd like for you to know.
Laying under 'ouses, hear the tiffs between the spouses –
I'm pleased I never 'Measured Up' as a beau.

'cos I'm the shortest in the Stump Setters Association –
Pedals in the truck adjust for both.
I never walk that far, 'cept from the house out to the car,
Maybe working under 'ouses *STUMPED* me growth.

Being the President of the Stump Setters Association,
I brought in a clause to protect us ' LITTLE MEN '.
You may say, " Does it matter,
They're out of sight, 'cept for the clatter."
Course it does ! The tallest chap is only four foot ten !

To be read in a soft *'Children's Hour'* voice.

Tarquin Helps His Daddy
(A Bonding Story)

Tarquin loves his bright-yellow tricycle, with it's new shiny bell – ding ! ding !

Tarquin's tricycle has a dicky seat at the back. Tarquin sits his favourite toys in the dicky seat, pretending his tricycle is a *big, big* bus !

Tarquin rides his tricycle on the garden path when it's a *big, big* bus ! making sure *never* to drive it on the grass !

Today Tarquin's bright-yellow tricycle will be a big bright-yellow truck – no rides for his favourite toys today !

Tarquin felt a teeny bit sorry for his toys, so he sat them all on cushions from his mummy's settee in the shade of the verandah. They could see Tarquin working hard from there, couldn't they ?

Tarquin wants to move stones and bricks today. Tarquin gave his large yellow truck a big drink of water as there is such a lot to do.

" Tarquin ! Tarquin ! Tarky !" (That's Tarquin's mummy calling him in to lunch. He's having a banana sandwich with crackly brown sugar and a small glass of milk.)

Tarquin has finished his lunch. He was quick, wasn't he ? That's because Tarquin wants to please his mummy and daddy.

Sometimes Tarquin's legs ache, moving stones and bricks. They are so heavy ! Tarquin's daddy has just arrived home from a job interview: no work for Tarquin's daddy today.

Tarquin's daddy went to the refrigerator. Holding open the door, he called to Tarquin's mummy: " ANY MORE STUBBIES, DARL ?"

Tarquin's mummy replied, " Not until your next payment, hon."

Instead she offered him a *BIG, BIG* mug of tea ! Tarquin's daddy walked out into his garden, sipping the large mug of tea.

When Tarquin's daddy saw how busy Tarquin had been, moving stones and bricks, Tarquin's daddy was very angry !

Waving his arms in the air (and the hot mug of tea !) spilling tea – hot tea ! – all down the front of his Jimmy Barnes tee shirt, he shouts to Tarquin's mummy.

" HAVE YOU SEEN WHAT THIS BLASTED KID'S BEEN DOING TODAY ? HAVEN'T YOU BEEN WATCHING HIM ? "

" Pardon, darling ? " purred Tarquin's mummy.

" LOOK !" shouted Tarquin's daddy (spilling more tea on his stone-washed jeans). He's moved all the ruddy bricks from the edge of the garden path and heaped them into the fish pond !"

Tarquin's mummy said, " Oh no ! I thought he was quiet. Can you remove them before you have to play snooker, dear ? "

Tarquin's daddy muttered something, then growled, " Struth, darl !"

Tarquin, holding onto his mummy's dress very tightly, said quietly, " Daddy is working hard now, isn't he, mummy ? "

Bye-bye.

The Evening I Dialled the BBC from Aussie
And heard:
" Hello, BBC Radio Two Help Line Here"

I'll tell you, when I heard that I'd got through
My mind went all asunder;
I forgot my number, 'blew' my name
But managed, " Er, yeh, it's me down under."

The machine then switched to 'programme mode',
I could only hang on and listen.
That female voice with creative flair,
It made my bald head glisten.

If I can help in your quest
For videos that make you bristle,
A floor plan of Harrods, bike clips or such
Forgotten music, I'll even whistle.

This and more I will answer.
We will go to a musical break,
When I come back it will be 'menus'
And a poser: Is it cod ? – Is it 'ake ?

Then of course next is my favourite: Bruce Bygraves.
He serenades me . . . in 'me' bower.
Perhaps I shouldn't broadcast this, but
Leaves me stone deaf for an hour.

I have here now, on this PC of mine
A 'MENU', cos this won't come cheap.
If you've written in, with faith in Her Majesty's post,
I have probably gone home for a sleep.

I have also two German antique nutcrackers,
A cat that's . . . *[pause]* . . . run away !
An Irishman ex-PAT in Melbourne –
I don't know what his name is today !

To NEEDLE and the lads in the limo,
Who delivered ' *Caught* ' by the Krays, to Chef Stan,
A retired lady in Essex asks:
" Would they deliver an inflatable man ?"

Now to the Popular Paper Backs,
'Air Fighters !' . . . who were randy
To the WAAFS who 'Propped Them High !'
By Bridget, Dot, and Mandy.

Also, . . . *IF* . . . your parrot's pegged it,
I have an idea here for Cy,
But if it's Peg that's legged it,
Taxidermist could be why.

I have a message for Lil Brady
Your equipment now is in.
For the students who are missing,
Your luck is running thin.

For any ANTIPODEANS
Whose UK contacts have now ' CARKED IT ',
You could always try me sometime –
Go on, . . . I dare you – ask it !

If I haven't covered every item
You may have had in mind,
I'll be with you all again next week
So see what you can find.

Oh ! . . . and a Cider Maker needs a CRUSHER
Preferably a professional . . . ex-madam
So please leave your name and number.
Good luck – Presenter Jan.